I AM A YAK

All you wanted to know about
Tibet's most beloved animal

NORBU C. KHARITSANG

PALJOR
PUBLICATIONS PRIVATE LTD.

I am a Yak. I want to tell you about myself because not many people know much about me. Here I am going to tell you a little bit about my life in Tibet.

Tibetans domesticated me about 3000 years ago, and ever since I have been living there. I live in Tibet because the cold climate is very good for me. I cannot live in a hot climate.

Tibet is located to the north of India and Nepal, south of Mongolia, and west of China. Average height of Tibet is about 4000 meters above sea level.

Tibetans are very peaceful and care-free people. They love me so much that sometimes I am used as a national symbol.

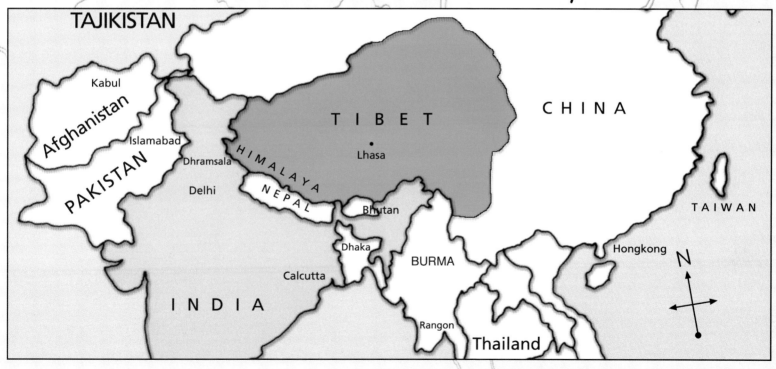

I look quite like an American buffalo, only a little smaller. My hair is black or brown or white. White is a rare and special colour.

Yaks that are born white do not carry loads or plough fields. They are trained and offered to high lamas for transportation, which is considered a privilege for a yak.

Everybody thinks I give milk and there is yak butter, but I don't give milk and there is no yak butter. I am the man of the house and do all the hard work. The word yak is reserved for me only. And a yak can be male only. My female partner is called dri (pro:dree). She is little smaller than me. She is the one who gives milk.

Tibetans churn milk to make butter and cheese in a barrel-like churner. Butter is primarily used by Tibetans to make offerings of butter lamp to the deities and to make Tibetan butter tea.

Just like in America and other parts of the world, Tibetans make a variety of cheese products too.

Tibet has a very cold and dry climate and not many vegetables grow there, so the Tibetans depend on yak meat and dairy products to supplement their food. They say there is no meat like yak meat.

Every family has a good supply of dried yak meat all the time. It provides them with a quick meal and is eaten in many different ways.

I am a very useful animal. Some people call me the beast of burden because I am very sure-footed and can carry big loads over high mountain passes in snow and ice.

I am the chief mode of transportation in tibet. I carry wool, salt, tea, and other finished goods to India, Nepal and China and, cotton, silk, glass and other finished products back to Tibet. I also carry pilgrims, farmers, monks, and traders and their belongings.

It is not just the traders I work for; I work for the nomads too. They depend on me and my female partner dri for their livelihood. The number of yaks, dri and sheep it owns often judges a nomad family's wealth. A family with ten thousand sheep and one thousand yaks and dri is considered extremely wealthy. Kar-ti Nag-tong, as they say.

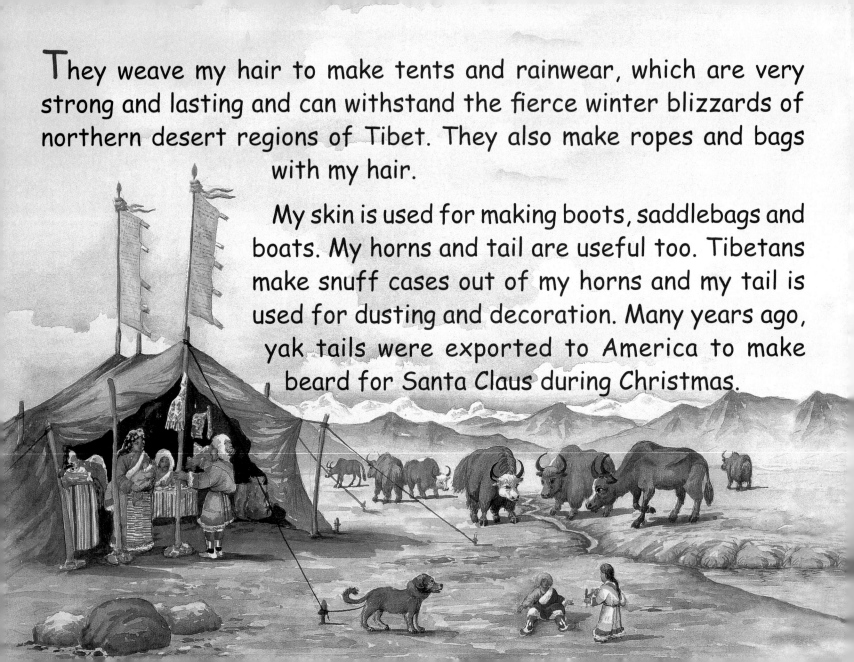

They weave my hair to make tents and rainwear, which are very strong and lasting and can withstand the fierce winter blizzards of northern desert regions of Tibet. They also make ropes and bags with my hair.

My skin is used for making boots, saddlebags and boats. My horns and tail are useful too. Tibetans make snuff cases out of my horns and my tail is used for dusting and decoration. Many years ago, yak tails were exported to America to make beard for Santa Claus during Christmas.

Along with my female partner dri and my cousin dzo we work for the farmers too. They also depend on us for a lot of their needs. Some farmers use yaks to plough fields though most used dzo.

I live for about 30 years. When I get old and cannot work anymore, my owner free or retire me to lead a work-free life. They consider me as a precious jewel of the family and treat me with great love and respect.

I am used in some other ways too. Tibetans, especially the nomads, use me as money. They exchange me with grains with the farmers or give me as wedding gifts.

So, now you know that I am not just a beast of burden as many of you call me. I am a very useful animal, probably the most useful of all the animals in the world.

Nowadays I live not only in Tibet. I live in Mongolia, Ladakh, in Northern India, and even in some parts of America too.